Feller

With a naturalist's sense of ecology and concision, Denton Loving weaves out of this world both allegory and immediacy, a place where you can be both hurt and healed, and where you must unbramble all the truths of living through this earth. Loving's precision of line and sentence, of image and sound, render poems where "Each bud swells and splits / and unfurls into leaves // and fruit. A tender explosion!" At once timely and timeless, *Feller* is a superbly striking and essential book.

—Matt W. Miller, author of *Tender the River*

Denton Loving makes lyric sense of complex issues in poem after poem in *Feller*, with his special blend of eco-poetics and earthly reason. Read this book for its verbal delights, even in heartbreak, where the speaker notes how "even a tree has desire," and is able to "praise the quake of the earth accepting its weight."

—Elaine Sexton, author of *Site Specific*

These poems shimmer and shapeshift like the dual meaning inherent in the collection's title. So too do the speakers in these poems, who are both vulnerable humans and conduits through which lyrical ecstasy passes. These are love poems, loss poems, poems that "open doors to new worlds." They refuse an easy sentimentality. *Feller* is defined by its abundance, by the "bright tapestry" of its intricately crafted sonic pleasures. Underlying the human "language of grief" and Loving's attentive reverence for the natural world is this music, which is always "a newly alive thing." Reading *Feller* is a transformative, joyful, loneliness-alleviating experience.

— Annie Woodford, author of *Where You Come from Is Gone*

Also by Denton Loving

Crimes Against Birds

Tamp

Seeking its Own Level: An Anthology of Writings about Water (editor)

Feller

Denton Loving

MERCER UNIVERSITY PRESS
Macon, Georgia

MUP/ P720

Published by Mercer University Press
1501 Mercer University Drive
Macon, Georgia 31207

29 28 27 26 25 5 4 3 2 1

Books published by Mercer University Press are printed on acid-free paper that meets the requirements of the American National Standard for Information Sciences—Permanence of Paper for Printed Library Materials.

Printed and bound in the United States.

This book is set in Adobe Garamond Pro.

Cover/jacket design by Burt&Burt.

ISBN 979-8-89736-000-0
Cataloging-in-Publication Data is available from the Library of Congress

for Walter, who always thinks of others

MERCER
UNIVERSITY

MERCER UNIVERSITY PRESS

Endowed by

TOM WATSON BROWN
and
THE WATSON-BROWN FOUNDATION, INC.

Contents

Prologue

Bluebird Dreams of Red Fox

And then as the eastern sky colors
like the skin of an over-ripened peach,
you appear—as if I conjured you—
pirouetting under my hemlock perch
with your death-kiss-is-beautiful kind
of allure—gangly, untamable, too proud—
and then you belly-creep home. I know
about your fatal fox magic, how you
open doors to new worlds, how you lure
hunters to fall in love with you. Could you
confound a bluebird, too, charming me
with your dance, pretending you can't
hear me when I'm singing your name?

Bluebird Dreams Red Fox Has Wings

I followed your tracks and flew back
in time to the mountain where
the Maker mined red clay to shape you.
I watched him kiss life into your lips,
and I prayed to be refashioned
like you with legs that glide like fire.
When the Maker refused my plea,
I begged instead to release the blood-
red Cardinal that beats inside your chest—
your fur burned into feathers—
so instead of always running ahead,
you could wing alongside me.

Bluebird Flies Too Close to Red Fox

Feverish, I find myself circling you
like the cow bride circles Jupiter.
Like Jupiter orbits the sun.
Your flame blazes bright as a star
but too much light blinds
and a bluebird is not a satellite.
Mid-revolution, my fever breaks
and I fly away. But not before
the feathers on my chest singe
the same burnt red as your fur.

Bluebird Removes Red Fox's Tooth

If I was apportioned to sky, and you
to land, why did the Maker shape me
to yearn for you? I was warned
unbridled love swallows whole,
but the pain remains.
                                        The fang
you buried in my neck's rusted feathers—
I've plucked it out and planted it
in the garden beside the remnants
of my need. Watered it with my blood.
Now, I wait and wonder what will grow.

I

Under the Chestnut Tree

What strange light filters through the sex
of a chestnut tree, leaves and catkins
blooming and softly falling, sickly-
sweet smell pressing into the warmth
of thick July. Whatever's dropped,
I heap into piles and set on fire.
Flames engulf, then slow to a smolder
that keeps the gnats at bay. Smell of smoke,
smell of sex. Sips of whiskey bewitch
shade into dusk the way burnt offerings
lure out stars and lovers.

Mount Athos

Around this mountain, shepherds drive flocks of goats,
the very young pulled in wagons. I'm given a billy

small enough to hold in one arm. The kid wrestles
alongside the fact of our imminent separation:

I will ferry across the Aegean to another island. You
will keep playing pilgrim, up one mountain, down another.

Before we part, feel the kid still soft from birth.
Feel it tremble, this newly alive thing between us.

Careful! There's a Man Inside the Belly of This Fish

Lost at sea, a man and his ship
slip through the teeth of a fish.

A young woman, hungry
and alone on an island,

wishes a wish.
With a flourish

of her hand,
the same fish—

swishes into her arms.
Her hunger shifts.

She sharpens
her knife,

slices a thin line
along the dorsal fin.

Light slits into the abyss,
reminds the shipman he's alive.

Chimney Birds

The squeaks are faint at first. Did you hear it too? I mute the television to zero in on the source. By late spring, there's no question. A smokestack hatchery for the untuned. The decibels rise as the sun reaches its zenith. So much noise. So many mouths clamoring, crying like babies in a cauldron, like prophets in the fire. You hear it, don't you? The growing force of their cries, fearless in their need. Pump up the volume on the news. Protesters in the streets could learn from these birds. I can't even tell what their picket signs are protesting. They can't match this pageantry and passion above the rafters. This is primordial. And to think that it comes from starlings or blackbirds: not a bird with showy colors worth looking up in the bird book, not a songbird. Just a bunch of baby passerines, squawking their blessings and curses, screeching more need than can ever be swallowed in such tiny beaks.

Albert Ulrey's X-ray Eyes

Albert Ulrey was the first person to describe the X-ray tetra

When I saw the tiny fish with its bones shining through
its diaphanous scales, I knew, with my eyes,

I could control the voltage required to increase electron speed
so I could see internal structures and diagnose maladies.

I could see the hundred species of tetras swimming the Amazon.
I could see the inner workings of the Helix Nebula.

With my extraordinary sight, I didn't need the tide to go out
to see who was swimming naked. I didn't have to heed

the Bible's advice to turn my eyes from nakedness,
to fish out my eye if it tempted me to sin—better, says scripture,

to live like a cyclops than for two eyes to drive us into hellfire.
But I never learned how much voltage it would take

to forgive my own sins, to reveal through my armature
the ponderous beasts swimming in my chest.

Budburst

Out of dormancy, sap rises
through winter-hardened vine.

Each bud swells and splits
and unfurls into leaves

and fruit. A tender explosion!
In this life, I train the canes,

and weed and water. I serve the grape
in the meager ways a man can.

In my next life, I don't want to
be the harvester or the harvest.

I want to be the budburst.
Those velvetlike lobes,

so diaphanous and sensuous
in their terrific unwinding—

Love Is Slippery

Eyes tangled, I was so tired on the last leg of my flight that I settled in 10C instead of 9C. The man assigned to 10C—bushy eyebrowed, wearing Volunteer-orange tennis shoes—was glad to switch. 9C was in the comfort zone and gave an extra half-inch of leg space. 9D was empty until a woman—the last to board the plane—claimed it, and we all flew north into the undying night. Perhaps because I heard one flight attendant say to another that love is slippery, or perhaps because I'm delusional about my role in the machine works of destiny, I wondered if I had taken the wrong seat so 9C and 9D might fall in love. But the two seemed to never speak, or not at least that I saw, and I watched even after the lights dimmed and the cabin grew dark. Once we landed, the couple uncoupled and stood on opposite sides of the baggage carousel. While we all waited for our luggage, I reconsidered the degrees to which love might, indeed, be slippery. Perhaps 9C and 9D had not been destined to meet. Or perhaps their meeting and falling in love had been only one possible destiny. Or perhaps the falling-in-love part might not come for another week or so, when 9D might bump into 9C while selecting oranges in a grocery store, and say, "Weren't you sitting next to me last week on that flight from Florida? I thought I recognized your shoes."

Tiffany Wants to Talk to Jesus

She means the man who looks
like Christ sitting at the last bar stool.
He doesn't look like the real Christ—
not a brown-skinned Middle Eastern man,
doing good—but a bearded European
like the masters painted. Cesare Borgia
with sleepy eyes. She gets like this
after too many Amaretto Sours.
She makes up names for strangers,
borrows their sunglasses and hats
when she's told it's time to leave.
Can we take Jesus with us, she asks.
Only in our hearts, baby girl.
Only in our hearts.

Landmark

Bill spills tipsy
into the Hermitage Café,
orders biscuits as big as a house
and thick sausage gravy.
I marvel at all the musicians
who've passed through this dive
with as much hope as hunger.
Always working third shift,
our waitress has served them all.
She holds her hollow mouth
like it ought to hold a cigarette
and I wish I had camels and a light.
Her body aches for nicotine
and because we all know
what it is to want something,
I crave it, too, if not for me,
for her, forgetting
about smoking ordinances
or long rivers of smoke
and the hazards of falling ashes
on my eggs fried over easy
and bacon extra crisp.

The Eagle and the Drone

My soul leapt, you said when you witnessed
the eagle attack the drone in mid-flight—
the drone's camera capturing its own finish,
the eagle cementing her reign of the sky.

When you read this, I think you'll know
the triumphant eagle is not a symbol
of America, and neither is the lost drone.
This is no polemic or war-time parable;

as far as I can tell, there's no clear wisdom
gained when we pit nature against technology.
I only know medicine men say eagles bring new vision—
like light through a lens passing obliquely

from air into a prism's flat panel of glass,
refracting and separating the sun's beams—
to help us understand our complicated past
and present, to guide us through the mysteries

of the future. That reminds me of the last trip
I made to visit you in Florida, when an eagle rose
from one of Highway 417's narrow strips
of median as you drove me to the airport in Orlando.

The eagle winged directly toward our windshield,
and we agreed it was a very good omen:
how she caught our eyes, how pure white her bald
head appeared before she flew into the morning sun.

Lake Sagatagan Summer

After evensong at the abbey, we walk circles
in the woods, weaving through deerflies

in kamikaze flights. The cerulean warbler
mates among these trees, we're told,

so we keep vigil for blue flickers in leaves.
So far, nothing. On half-submerged logs

turtles perch like hard-shelled gods—
We canoe to the deepest part of the lake

before we can talk about who we were
before the other existed as witness.

Night descends, and we have to compete
with the liturgy of loons,

but here, surrounded by water, by darkness,
is the only safe place to tell the truth.

Lock the Moon

Let's lock the moon where it sits
in the eastern sky, as two raccoons
wrestle over cat food, knock about
the water bowl, and leave tracks

that vanish in the dew. Everywhere,
fireflies engage in their own
urgent fracas. The cats ignore it all.

Let's divide the sky into five quarters.
On a plate of gold, I will cut the flesh
from the stone and serve it to you.

I was reborn the night we met,
a night like this with fireflies
and trains traveling cross-continent.
But in what direction do we move?

Climb this tree with me, my love.
Place one foot here. Push yourself
up, and I will pull. Ignore the moon
always laughing at desire.

Rituals for Calling Fish

Never speak of fishing, or whistle on the water,
lest the fish hear you and swim away.

Never let your shadow fall on the water
lest the fish see you and swim away.

Whatever your bait is—worm, minnow, crayfish,
squid—spit on it, and the fish won't swim away.

Offer a sip of good beer to thirsty river spirits
so they don't push the fish to swim away.

Test your hook against your skin, christening
metal with blood, so the fish won't swim away.

Break the water with your cupped hand and whisper
a dream, and the fish won't swim away.

What's a small sacrifice of beer, blood, or desire
if it means the fish won't swim away?

If you have a beloved, steal a kiss to prove
you won't let a keeper swim away.

Do You Hear the Cicadas?

And how about the whippoorwill?
I hear him late into night, nearly
four decades gone from these
wooded foothills but returned
to sound his warrior song
whip-poor-weel, whip-poor-weel—
turf warning as well as mating call—
a blast that rips through my sleep
some nights and leaves me to lie
awake and wonder about choices
I've made. And I wonder why
the whippoorwill was so long silent—
probably too much pesticide,
not enough moths and beetles,
all the too-usual reasons.
What makes him think things
will be different this time? What
calls him back? What sustains
this small nightjar's blind bravery?

II

The Moon Was Only a Rumor

Beneath the canopy, vast darkness
transports me back to sticky Kentucky

summers of my youth when I packed my bag
with more books and bourbon than clothes,

and drifted through old-growth forests,
feeling my way with my feet and a little luck.

Sometimes I heard travelers on the path ahead.

Their voices—like faint beams of starlight
bouncing through the trees—felt so real.

I tried to latch on to them before
they attached to the trees like leaves,

leaving me in more darkness and with a silence
inside me that I never meant to carry home.

Simulation Hypothesis

Five days with no word when your message arrives:

Been in the wilderness in Botswana, camping
with lions and hippos outside the tent.

I return to the Africa mapped in my imagination,
wallpapered in glossy *National Geographic* photos—

just enough data to create unconvincing simulations
that question your existence. And our distance

hits me as my mind travels the roads you've taken
to reach remote tracts with the best wildlife. At night

I wonder if you share your tent, and with whom,
and if you mean it when you end your texts,

Wish you were here.

Returning

My heart is divided,
split in devotion
to where I am
and where I want to be.
My wish to sew
my own life line with
a single, simple thread
is thwarted by these
rolling Appalachians,
their foothills and low reliefs.
So my path unwinds
like cable-stitch
that twins and twists
but never breaks.

Letter to Jeremy Wade

Last night I watched you dangle in a cage
while a school of bull sharks circled round,
just so you could shine a light into their eyes—
an experiment to see if their ocular tissue—
the tapetum lucidum—might glow devil red.
But only a yellow glare reflected back—
eerie in its own right. *Tapetum lucidum*—
Latin for bright tapestry—like the Bayeux
with its ancient world woven inside, and all
those lives depicted in thread—except *this*
bright tapestry gives some animals superior
night vision. God knows why I get sucked in
as you interview villagers across the globe
who pause their digging in some river's clay
to recall the night the monster with the red eyes
dragged a lamb or shoat—or maybe a child—
underwater. I wish you would tell me instead
about the phoenix, the quetzalcoatl, the griffin—
magical beasts with the kind of oracular sight
that can see meaning in waters far murkier
than where your monsters navigate. Oh, Jeremy!
When you dive into mysterious rivers, do you
ever wonder about your soul? If I looked
into the bright tapestry of the phoenix's eyes,
would the light of my half-lived life reflect at all?

When We Were Sheep

after Caki Wilkinson

We were typical.
We escaped all fences
while the shepherd slept.

We stomped his fields of leeks
eating as we went,
tromping what we left.

We kept bad hours.
When the shepherd gave chase
we climbed a steeper peak.

When things looked bleakest,
we crept home in the dark.
We played at being meek.

When you reaped our wool
and ate our young,
we turned the other cheek.

Photo of False Bay

You've captured shades of blue I don't have
names for—in the water and sky, in cliff shadows
and the low, sandy strips of False Bay's beach,

and I almost miss your caption: *outside Fish Hoek*
over the mountain from where someone turned
across traffic and knocked me down with his car.

I prefer the way Dias first referred to it in 1488:
the gulf between the mountains. I know
all about the gaps between two bodies of rock,

how tectonic plates drift together and rift apart
like the car that kissed you and struck you down.
Whatever draws me to you knocks me down too.

And You Too

after Agnar Artúvertin

And you too shall be full,
you who devour the meat of the mountain.

And you too shall be honored,
you who wash out your underwear in motel bathrooms.

And you too shall know comfort,
you who crawl under cold sheets each night alone.

And you too shall be rich,
you who abandon what you most love.

Some Gods

Some gods are grateful for any recognition, any whisper
of their names in night's quiet darkness.

Some gods are greedy and want starring roles in dreams
that unfurl in night's quiet darkness.

Some gods balance the scales, rolling us uphill, pushing us down,
gifting pleasure and pain in night's quiet darkness.

Some gods linger in strange beauty, like the first snow to fall
on our gravestones in night's quiet darkness.

Some gods ascend great heights where it's easier to see how,
in night's quiet darkness, staying and going are the same.

Breach

All our conversations circle back to desire,
you wanting to know what I want,

using desire *singular* as if I have only one
when I'm normally drowning in them.

I sailed once to South Africa's Western Cape
to witness southern right whales breaching.

I wasn't impressed at the penguin beach,
but the baleen mothers and their calves

breaking the horizon, splashing salt spray,
quickened my pulse—

The whole pod swam closer to observe us.
I wanted to dive in, to give myself

to their body of water,
but my guide held me back, reminding me

the ocean we desire might desire us
to live a little longer on dry land.

When the One You Want Won't Love You Back

Plant fields of California poppies and cosmic orange cosmos.
Remember the heart deceives.

Think how the goldfinch, nuthatch and chickadee feast
on blue thistle, eating around prickly leaves.

My Spirit

after Frank O'Hara

I don't dress down all the time. Nor do I dress
to perfection to feed the cat or cut the lawn,
to write a poem or pick up groceries. When I
worked in an office, I wore long sleeves,
a tie, slacks and a jacket. I didn't hate it.
But I'm more me in jeans and a tee shirt,
functional clothes that don't need changing
before I light the grill, work the cows or plant
a row of tomato seedlings. But my inner snob
draws a few lines my inner slob dares not cross.
No bootcut jeans. No holes in the knees. No
acid washes or drop crotches. For tees, I require
cotton blends to keep my sleeves and neckline
from losing shape. I want my shirts the way
I want my spirit. To not tear when pulled tight.
Able to stretch and snap back.

The Opposite of Love Is Indifference

When you ask
if I hate you now,

if there's any love
left, I remember

my ninth grade
earth science teacher

who taught me
about water's stickiness.

The way it clings
to skin. The way

it holds and grasps—
the same as the past.

What I feel
refuses to be

rushed. What I felt
refuses to forget.

Yes, the bulk
streams away,

but the rest
collects, takes

its time
to drip.

Letter to My Lover as Abraham Lincoln

Just once, I wish you'd put yourself under my stovepipe.
I passed through airport security only to find you waiting
at the gate with luggage and a ticket for the seat next to mine.
Wheels down safe in Florida, I tried to lose you by slipping
into the Dali Museum where I contemplated Salvador's
naked wife Gala in cruciform windows, forever contemplating
the Mediterranean. As I squinted in pleasure at her beauty,
your face snapped into view. You had been there all along,
my escape as false as the mystery of identity. Your generals
could only dream of the subtle ways you invade the enemy
consciousness with your myths of honesty and homespun wit,
as commonplace as pancakes at the pancake house,
as tireless as termites over millennia, consecrated in the church
of illusions. Yes, your Dali magic has some charm, turning
elephants into obelisks, sailors into saints, water into wine.
But honestly, I wish you'd slash the miraculous manipulations.
Being raised, fed and nurtured in your cult, sometimes water
is all I want. I have worshipped at your altar, so I feel qualified
to tell you: this is why so many are unnerved by surrealism.
According to *Scientific American*, we need as few as 252 pixels
to identify the face of someone we know and possibly love.
Or once did. The real question is how I break through the layers
of optical scales to know myself. That's all I'm trying to do.
No need to feel so threatened. Let's each do our own thing.
You should buy a digital camera and shoot some nature photos.
I'll practice being a person who spends all his pennies.

Salt Pan Selfies

Mixed among photos of zebras and wildebeests,
there are two of you in the salt flats of Botswana—

The first only a silhouette on parched moonscape,
a foreign sun shining on alabaster, elongating
your legs as if you're roaming the desert on stilts.

The other, a reflection in a Range Rover's mirror.
So much distance between us already, and yet—
your face is blocked by the camera in your hand.

The Word of the Day Is *Largesse*

From the Latin *largus*, meaning not just big but *abundant,*
generous: I am blessed by the *largesse* of those who came

before me, benefactors bestowing aid and alms, though
no one these days gives *alms*, another ancient word,

this one from Greek, akin to *compassion*. After Artemis
transformed Hippocrates' daughter into a sea serpent,

men seeking the *largesse* of her father lined up to free
the girl with their kiss. Yet, those men fled the serpent's

scaly mouth. Her split tongue. Her poisoned breath. Did I
mention those men each died soon after? The moral is,

if you can't love with *compassion,* just get out. Leave.
I've been reading mythology and backbone recipes

like a man sizing up a bear. The backbone, or what's left
after the ribs are cut, is prized for its flavor and tenderness.

Pork is good, but bear is better, makes delicious broth, soup
and stir fries. It was the only meat Davy Crockett would eat.

He killed hundreds of bears, leaving his wife for weeks to hunt.
To prepare your own backbone, ensure your cleaver is sharp.

Hack the meat into small pieces. Sauté *generous, abundant*
amounts of aromatics. Brown the meat and mix together.

Savor. Be sure you have plenty to give away.

III

Thirst

This is the longest winter—the coldest, snowiest, loneliest.
More time to marvel how the years stretch

since you've asked about my life or since we've shared
a meal at the same table, what smoldered between us

no longer igniting, edging perilously close to its fuse.
Three years since I've heard your voice, pondered why

you hum out of key though I know you sing so well—
Were you troubled by last night's ice storm?

Did you feed the birds as I did? Did you watch them
from your bedroom window? Three years later—

a thousand days—I can see a Cardinal and not think
of you. It was only rain here—so much farther South—

a few pellets of sleet, not worth mentioning
if we were speaking, but we aren't. So I return

to my reading: poems, stories, essays about water.
Even my mail is about streams and rivers, lakes

and oceans, sometimes swelling, sometimes deceiving.
I immerse myself in water, though below ground

my well has frozen. I shower at friends', carry bottles home
to drink until the next thaw. It's only January, the worst

of winter still to come. When you don't have water,
it's all you think about. My thirst jolts me awake in the night.

Sleep Apnea

Five seconds or less. Regular as—
a clock, I almost said, but not a clock. I need

a horologist to suggest a timepiece less reliable
than Swiss works, less cumbersome than sundials

and hourglasses. I need some custom-made
instrument to measure irregular amounts of time,

and bursts of air pressure as unpredictable as grief,
the kind that sometimes pops up alongside joy.

It's not up to me when I breathe, nor how deeply.
Nor why some ghosts refuse to leave.

They watch me sleep, counting the seconds
between each breath, waiting

for the long pause to grow a little longer.
In the perilous silence, they grow a little stronger.

I Can’t Quit Looking at Other Men’s Shoes

In restaurants, airports, I’m seduced by nubuck loafers,
dark brown brogues with double monk straps, capped toe derbies,

I marvel in the gym at sneakers with visible air in the heels,
propulsive plates, bright textiles woven from recycled ocean plastic.

Don’t get me started on utility boots.
One day, I’ll be called out: *My eyes are up here, dude.*

What worries me more is what my poor shoe-manship reveals:
an unstylish man, unsure, underconfident, broken-soled.

Feller

This is the white oak that grew among other oaks and beech,
pine and hemlock. This is the tag that marks the tree.
This is the saw with whirring blades. This is the sawdust
that thickens the air. Praise the machine and the task it achieves.

This is the creak of the trunk splitting. This is the fracturing
of fibrous limbs as they bend and break. Praise the thunder
of the falling. Praise the quake of the earth accepting its weight.

This is the log hauled to the sawmill, cut into lumber, measured
by board feet. Praise the planks that will shape a dwelling.

This is the crown of the tree. These are the branches left to rot.
This is the wood's cellulose and lignin that replenish the soil.
These are the fungi, the beetles and the earthworms that flourish
in the oak's remains. Praise decay and decomposition.

This is the feller who brought the tree down. Praise the worker
and the work of felling trees. Praise the quickening pulse
and the flowing blood.

This is the first green leaf from last year's acorn, taking root.
This is the light that enters the woods and cleanses the wound.

Praise the wood and the woods. Praise the light, praise the wound.

Letter to J.

I've long feared hearing my name called in a crowd exactly
the way your mother called mine in that coffee shop
on Bloomsbury. She was unrecognizable. But I knew you
even with your hand clamped over your mouth. You sat
beside your kids, silent and still as a viper in plain sight.
It felt like a trick when I looked in your eyes, said your name.
Your staccato hello was wide enough to see the toothless
cavern of your mouth, the unexpected hollow of your life.
Drug guides say self-loathing causes self-destructive behavior.
In high school you called my house so often I invented the phrase
that's my name, don't wear it out. We tied up, twisted our parents'
phone lines, pretending we were *hella fly*, perfecting the practice
of 90's teen life. Now, I wonder, could I have been kinder?
Dear crank mouth, dear meth head, dear girl I used to know,
you were a smart girl. How did we let this happen? The coal fields
have been burning for decades now, and users sprout in the ash.
We are what anthropologists call a self-contained people,
as if these mountains were islands in the clouds for the condemned.
Please don't take what I say as pride. Maybe you've had happiness
I will never know. I hope you'll have more. As for me, I have
no children. I've only known broken love. I spend most of my time
alone. You prove it's dangerous to walk around our hometown,
our lives crashing backwards, choices barreling down
the mountain, the wreckage difficult to ignore.

Dodgeball

I've reached an age where I feel ashamed
when I give in to sleep, a new layer of disgrace.

My regrets have always flowed like silt, collected
and accumulated. Imagine a riverbank with strata

chronicled by humiliation: tiers for weight
I've gained, seams of coal for clichéd heartache.

Notice all the marbled deposits for wasted time
and money, mislaid opportunities, lost campaigns.

Some failings fossilize like a seabed of trilobites
while this wasp preserved in amber for ninety-nine

million years is a precise memory from first grade:
I didn't dodge, and the ball struck me in the face.

No One Lives at Xanadu

How did Didion know about our snow-covered January
in Vermont? I broke in new boots and wore a blue hat
a friend knitted to keep my head warm. We danced late
into the night and carried the music with us into the cold
dark—exhausted like after a day digging and planting.
Past carriage barn and pond, we hiked through sleeping
hayfield and chose the shortcut through the woods.
The pond—frozen when we arrived—thawed and refroze.
June's geese had flown south and didn't care. Such magic
comes and goes. Even the best spells must be recast.

Midnight at 3 Crow Bar

A box truck pulls into 3 Crow's parking lot;
on the patio, we can't hear each other speak.
The truck's back door rolls up revealing disco lights
from a traveling band taking over 11th Street.

The lead singer bounces his hips, entreats us
to dance with him, to feel the music's pulse,
but the four-on-the-floor beat with the heavy kick
comes from a drummer deep in the truck—

an intergalactic knight with a neon helmet
and a visor that glistens like frosted glass,
another ghost in the East Nashville night—
and I feel how the future will reshape the past.

Optography

If it's true an image affixes like a negative
to our eyes after life's gloam turns dark,

then I will still see the trace of mountain.
Of slope, escarpment, cliff line and crest.

Of coal-robbed wounds where trees won't grow.
Of hollowed faults and white rock walls.

Mountains are so good for our souls,
their durability might be mistaken for love.

But when my body returns to dust,
I'll be no more mourned than a fallen hawk.

The hard quartzose sandstone of this range—
once raised heavenward by tectonic thrust—

will remain as stoic and unmoved
by my passing as it has stayed untouched

by the ages of wind and rain
that long ago eroded all the softer rock.

Letter to Rilke

You say to have *patience with everything unsolved*
in my heart and *to cherish the questions*, but I'm
bursting with so much that is unnamed and unsolvable.
I've not yet learned to treasure locked doors, rooms
I've not been given access to. I've not yet learned
to be brave in the face of the *inexplicable*. Last month,
my sister died suddenly, and I have yet to mourn.
She was forty-seven years old, even younger than you
when ulcers filled your mouth instead of poems.
Yesterday, I flashed my hazards and stopped my car
on a busy road to help a box turtle reach the other side—
a small gesture for a species that has endured this earth
for two hundred million years—before lizards, before
crocodiles, long before there were snakes in Eden. Think
of all the strange tongues she has known and forgotten.
Is a language for grief one of them? Is she, like us,
unspeakably alone? The turtle reveals nothing.
Last week, flying from LaGuardia, I sat in a window seat
in an exit row. I considered the emergency door,
those few inches of carbon fiber composite separating me
from clouds and sky. An airtight lock and latch. Another
door with *the future* on one side, and me on the other,
afraid to die and afraid not to, which is to say, afraid to live.

Outside San Miguel

Highland breezes blew through your new backyard
outside Montañas de San Miguel. The coolest
August evening either of us could remember,
but we lost our clothes, submersed ourselves
in the distortion of underwater light and shadow.

You didn't mind the cold, but I shivered
as the water closed over our heads.
Afterwards,
driving north on the interstate long after midnight,
searching for a reported blue moon
through drifting fog, I carried with me the memory
of my teeth on the slope of your clavicle—
how I loved that word and still do,
how I still dream of that slight ridge
rising from the topography of your body.

The moon never revealed itself through the mist.
No roads wound back to those mountains.

My letter returned in the mail
with no forwarding address—
further evidence of your myth,
a lost continent the water closed over.

Marcescence

Strange how the Latin meant only to fade
but now the word—reserved for botany—

means to wither but also persist.
To dim but linger. Dwindle but endure.

A term for trees like the beech that hold
thinly bronzed leaves long into winter,

awaiting that secret signal to wake.
Yes, we know what the beech needs—

warmer days, a change in the light—
but how much, exactly how much?!

Strange how even a tree has desires.
Strange how until something new grows,

what no longer serves will cling.

I Am a Small Whorled Pogonia

after Lauren Davis

Some say I reveal myself
only after decade-long gaps.

Others say I'm only legend.

The truth is I—the rarest
of orchids—hide well.

And only the precise light
of a broken forest canopy

can coax me up to unfurl
my five spiral leaves.

The worthy, alone, will find
a way to witness my bloom.

Let botanists explain how

flowers without nectar or scent
still find a way to bear fruit.

How to Raise an Obelisk

With rope and sand and a touch of genius,
experts say, but don't get ahead of yourself.

The first trick is to recognize that ray
of light fossilized deep in the mountain.

Think red granite. Think white limestone
to glimmer in the distance. Draw ochre-

colored lines to direct scores of carvers
with their chisels and picks, their levers

and water-soaked wooden wedges. Once cut,
polish the rock face with fine-grit sand.

Smooth the surface to please the god
embedded within. Engrave the shaft

with battle stories. Embellish and repeat,
and paint with hard-won blood. Yes,

raising the needle is easier than historians
lead us to believe. And beside the point.

The Octopus School of Poetry

Yes, that they have three hearts is remarkable.
So too, the way they navigate man-made mazes.

That their eight arms simultaneously perform
separate tasks. That they can unscrew jar lids

even when they're trapped inside the glass.
But of all the strange facts, I can't get past

their ability to squirt jets of black ink,
theatrical for sure, but an effective tactic

to distract a hungry eel or seal or albatross—
not unlike the poem, shooting fireworks

to ward off what haunts us. Such a nifty trick.
Almost worth the burden of those extra hearts.

Rosy Maple Moth

Resting from the rough work of pollination
and procreation, moths the size of my thumbnail

pepper the door jam and deck boards outside
my house. They await the imminent night shift

to take flight again, in some way the same way
I am resting from jagged desire, and I wonder

why I've never seen—or never noticed—
the strange beauty of their wooly yellow heads

and thoraxes, their silky pink and yellow wings,
their lives as luscious and as fleeting as my own.

Notes

Mount Athos, page X: Mount Athos is a mountain in northeastern Greece. The name translates in some languages as "Holy Mountain." In Greek mythology, Athos was a giant who fought Poseidon. One tradition tells that Athos threw a rock into the Aegean Sea that became the mountain. Another tradition tells that Poseidon used the mountain to trap and bury the giant.

Albert Ulrey's X-ray Eyes, page X: Albert Brennus Ulrey (1860-1932) was a marine biologist who served as Professor of Biology and Zoology at the University of Southern California from 1901 to 1929. He was the first person to describe *Pristella maxillaris*, a small freshwater fish with a translucent body.

Landmark, page X: Hermitage Café was an iconic location in Nashville, Tennessee, frequented by countless musicians and country music legends for almost 32 years. It closed on October 31, 2021.

Photo of False Bay, page X: Fish Hoek is a coastal town in South Africa. Portuguese mariner and explorer Bartolomeu Dias was the first European navigator to round the southern tip of Africa. He originally referred to False Bay as "the gulf between the mountains." Later sailors confused the bay with Table Bay to the north, and thus the name False Bay was coined and stuck.

Letter to Jeremy Wade, page X: Jeremy Wade is a British biologist, angler, author, and television presenter known for exploring rivers and lakes seeking creatures from local folklore.

The Word of the Day Is Largesse, page X: Hippocrates' daughter being transformed into a dragon by the goddess Diana comes from *The Travels of Sir John Mandeville*, written in the 14th century. The Mandeville story is largely considered a variation of the more common European folk legend of Melusine, usually depicted as a woman who is a serpent from the waist down.

My Spirit, page X: This poem was inspired by Frank O'Hara's poem "My Heart," published in *The Collected Poems of Frank O'Hara.*

When We Were Sheep, page X: This poem was inspired by Caki Wilkinson's poem "When We Were Shepherds," originally published by *The Nation.*

And You Too, page X: This poem was inspired by Agnar Artúvertin's poem "And You Too," translated from Faroese to English by Matthew Landrum, published in *The Lonesome Savior: Hin Einsami Frelsarin.*

Letter to My Lover as Abraham Lincoln, page X: This poem describes Salvador Dali's 1977 mixed media artwork, *Lincoln in Dalivision.* At a distance of 20 meters or more, the pixelated image of President Lincoln is visible. When viewed from a closer distance, Lincoln's visage is transformed—somewhat like a photomosaic image—into an earlier Dali painting depicting his wife, *Gala Contemplating the Mediterranean Sea.*

No One Lives at Xanadu, page X: This title paraphrases an often-quoted line from "A Trip to Xanadu," Joan Didion's 1968 essay about visiting William Randolph Hearst's San Simeon castle. Didion's original quote says, "To think of 'living' there was to reduce the miraculous to the mundane; one does not 'live' at Xanadu."

Optography, page X: Quartzose sandstone is particularly notable in the formation of Cumberland Mountain near Cumberland Gap, Tennessee. Quartzose sandstone is harder and more resistant to erosion than many other types of sedimentary rocks. That resistance to weathering helped create Cumberland Mountain's rugged topography.

Letter to Rilke, page X: The italicized words and phrases within the poem are borrowed from Bohemian-Austrian poet Rainer Maria Rilke's collection of ten letters written to Franz Xaver Kappus, published as *Letters to a Young Poet*.

Outside San Miguel, page X: Like many legendary or mythical locations, including the miraculous Xanadu referenced by Joan Didion, Montañas de San Miguel is a place of magnificent splendor but unmappable and, therefore, often unattainable.

I Am a Small Whorled Pogonia, page X: The small whorled pogonia, *Isotria medeoloides*, sometimes referred to as "little five leaves," is a member of the orchid family that grows in forests and woodlands. Listed as a federal endangered species since 1982, the small whorled pogonia is mostly threatened by collection and habitat alteration. This poem was inspired by Lauren Davis's poem "I Am a New Caledonian Owlet-Nightjar," published in her collection *Home Beneath the Church*.

Acknowledgments

The author gratefully acknowledges the following publications where poems in this collection first appeared, sometimes in slightly different form, and especially the editors of these publications:

I-70 Review: "The Opposite of Love is Indifference"

Appalachian Places Magazine: "Feller," "Optography," and "Returning"

Delta Poetry Review: "Breach," "Careful! There's a Man Inside the Belly of This Fish," "How to Raise an Obelisk," "Letter to Rilke," "Rosy Maple Moth," "Tiffany Wants to Talk to Jesus" as "2:00 a.m. at 3 Crow Bar," and "The Word of the Day Is Largesse"

Ecotone: "Under the Chestnut Tree"

Exit 7: "The Eagle and the Drone" and "Landmark," previously published as "After Leaving 3 Crow Bar"

The Freeman: "Thirst"

Harvard Divinity Bulletin: "Letter to J." and "Mount Athos"

I Thought I Heard a Cardinal Sing, Ohio's Appalachian Voices: "Do You Hear the Cicadas?"

Kestrel: "My Spirit"

museum of americana: "Albert Ulrey's X-Ray Eyes" and "Lake Sagatagan Summer"

Peauxdunque Review: "When We Were Sheep"

Poetry South: "Bluebird Dreams of Red Fox" and "Bluebird Dreams Red Fox Has Wings"

Salvation South: "Chimney Birds," "Letter to Jeremy Wade," "Lock the Moon," "Love Is Slippery," "Marcescence," "The Moon Was Only a Rumor," "The Octopus School of Poetry," and "Rituals for Calling Fish"

Sheila-Na-Gig: "I Am a Small Whorled Pogonia"

Southern Poetry Review: "Sleep Apnea"

The Tishman Review: "And You Too" and "Outside San Miguel"

Tupelo Quarterly: "Letter to My Lover as Abraham Lincoln"